Dazzling
Decimals

Lisa Arias

ROurke
Educational Media

rourkeeducationalmedia.com

Scan for Related Titles
and Teacher Resources

Before Reading:

Building Academic Vocabulary and Background Knowledge

Before reading a book, it is important to tap into what your child or students already know about the topic. This will help them develop their vocabulary, increase their reading comprehension, and make connections across the curriculum.

1. *Look at the cover of the book. What will this book be about?*
2. *What do you already know about the topic?*
3. *Let's study the Table of Contents. What will you learn about in the book's chapters?*
4. *What would you like to learn about this topic? Do you think you might learn about it from this book? Why or why not?*
5. *Use a reading journal to write about your knowledge of this topic. Record what you already know about the topic and what you hope to learn about the topic.*
6. *Read the book.*
7. *In your reading journal, record what you learned about the topic and your response to the book.*
8. *After reading the book complete the activities below.*

Content Area Vocabulary
Read the list. What do these words mean?

addends

annex

commutative property
    of multiplication

denominators

difference

digit

dividend

divisor

factor

minuend

product

quotient

remainder

sum

After Reading:

Comprehension and Extension Activity

After reading the book, work on the following questions with your child or students in order to check their level of reading comprehension and content mastery.

1. *Explain how you read numbers with decimals. (Summarize)*
2. *What is the divisor? (Summarize)*
3. *When have you used decimals outside of school work? (Text to self connection)*
4. *When adding or subtracting, why do you need to line up the decimals? (Summarize)*
5. *Why don't you need to line up decimals when multiplying? (Asking questions)*

Extension Activity

Decimals are everywhere! Your parents encounter decimals each time they go shopping. Don't think they do? Grab a grocery ad from any grocery store and plan a meal for your family. You need to include a meat, two sides, a drink, and dessert. Write down the cost for each item. Look carefully as some items, such as meat, are sold by the pound. This means you need to multiply the number of pounds you want to purchase by the price per pound advertised. Add your items together to get your total cost. Be aware of the decimal rules while you are adding your items. What would your dinner cost for your family?

Table of Contents

What Are Decimals?

Decimals are the fractional parts found at the start of our number system.

A decimal point separates whole numbers from their fractional parts.

Whole					Parts		
thousands	hundreds	tens	ones	decimal point	tenths	hundredths	thousandths
	,				•			

Decimals are fractions based on ten,
so their **denominators** are never, ever written.

$$0.8 = \frac{8}{10} \qquad 0.4 = \frac{4}{10} \qquad 0.7 = \frac{7}{10}$$

$$0.35 = \frac{35}{100} \qquad 0.70 = \frac{70}{100} \qquad 0.55 = \frac{55}{100}$$

$$0.278 = \frac{278}{1,000} \qquad 0.499 = \frac{499}{1,000} \qquad 0.012 = \frac{12}{1,000}$$

Check It Out!

The zero in front of a decimal is only there to help you notice the decimal point.

Read Decimals

Reading decimals is really cool,
as long as you know the last place value.

Let's give it a try and correctly read the decimal
.207

Step #1 Read the digits to the right of the decimal just as you would a whole number.

Step #2 Say the place value of the last **digit** in the decimal.

Step #3 You are through because that is all you do!

$$0.207$$

tenths
hundredths
thousandths

Two hundred seven thousandths

Check It Out!

Ignore the decimal and the zero to the left of it.

Read Mixed Decimals

A **mixed decimal** has three parts. Let's take a look at how to read each part.

105.86

Whole-number part | Decimal Point | Decimal Part

Reading a mixed decimal is easy to do.
Just follow these steps all the way through.

Step #1 Read the whole number to the left of the decimal.

Step #2 Say and for the decimal.

Step #3 Read the digits to the right of the decimal just as you would a whole number.

Step #4 End by saying the place value of the last digit in the decimal.

↓

105.86

One hundred five and eighty-six hundredths

24.578 *is twenty four and five hundred seventy-eight thousandths.*
9,001.14 *is nine thousand one and fourteen hundredths.*
0.02 *is two hundredths.*
0.010 *is ten thousandths.*

Decimal Models

Decimal models are just the right tool
to compare values of decimals for me and you.

Hundredths Decimal Model

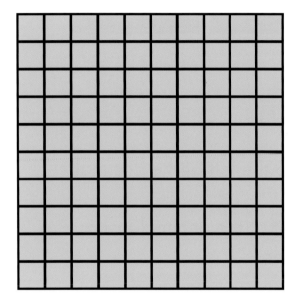 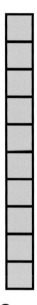 

One Whole   One Tenth   One Hundredth

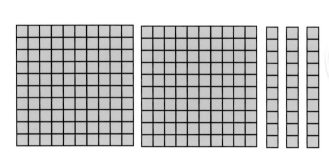

2.3
Two and three tenths

Check It Out!

One whole is 100 parts. 10 tenths make a whole. 100 hundredths make a whole.

6

Answers:

3.76 Three and seventy-six hundredths

0.42 Forty-two hundredths

2.06 Two and six hundredths

0.09 Nine hundredths

2.3 Two and three tenths

What is the decimal number for each model?

Add Decimals

Models are helpful tools for adding decimals when you're in school.

Add: 0.42 + 0.33

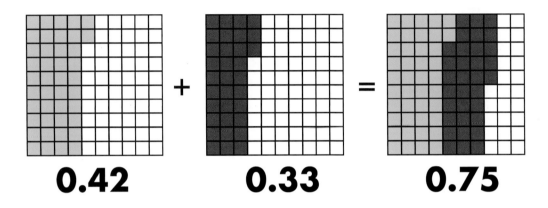

0.42   **0.33**   **0.75**

Add: 0.6 + 0.12

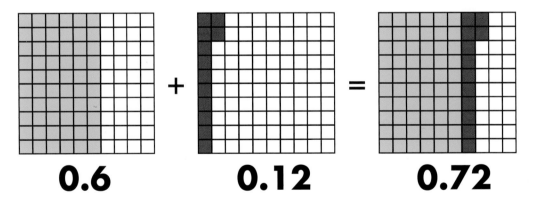

0.6   **0.12**   **0.72**

Models are key to help you see
how lining up the decimal dot
keeps all of the values in the right spot.

Find the **sum** of each model.

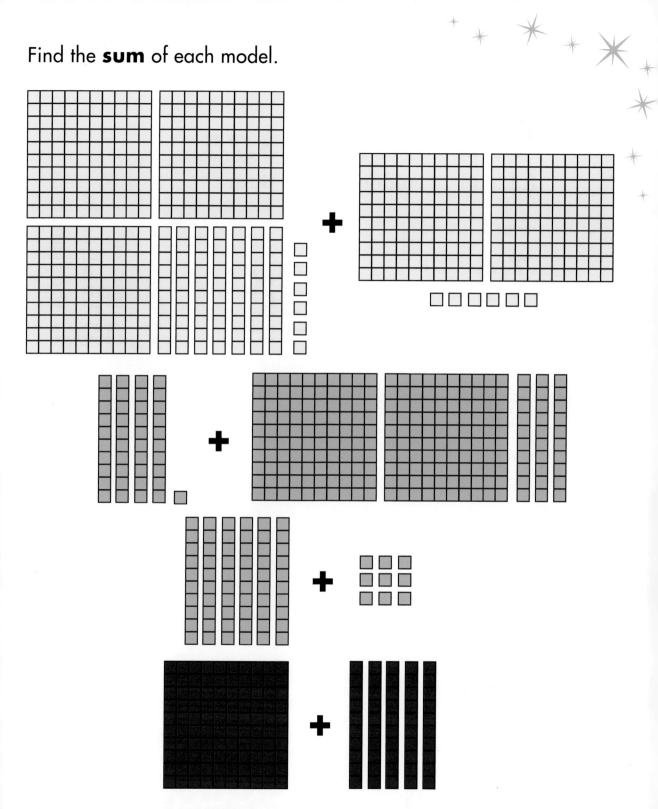

When adding decimals, line up each **addend's** decimal dot to keep their values in the right spot.

$$7.4 + 6.35 = 13.75$$

Addend   Addend   Sum

```
  7.4            7.4☺
+6.35          +6.35
_____         _____
```

Ones | tenths | hundredths | thousandths

7.4☺☺

If you like, **annex** zeros with faces to fill empty spaces.

After adding, drop the decimal dot straight down to place correctly in the sum.

```
  7.4
+6.35
_____
13.75
```

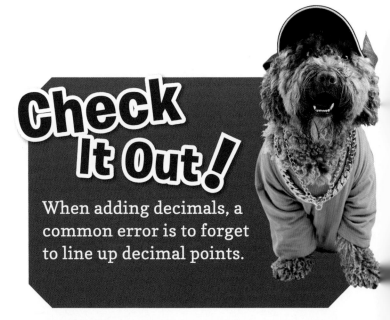

Check It Out!

When adding decimals, a common error is to forget to line up decimal points.

15 = 15.

Where are the decimals in whole numbers? Put on your glasses and you will see, there is a decimal hidden behind me.

Find each sum. Remember to include the decimal point in your answer!

12.5 + 8

6.75 + 12.6

0.01 + 0.1

19.01 + 58.8

37 + 0.07

Subtract Decimals

Before we begin, check the parts of a subtraction equation.

1.57 – 0.32 = 1.25
Minuend Subtrahead Difference

To model subtraction, start with a model of the **minuend**.

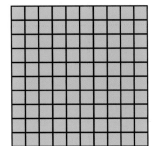 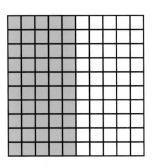 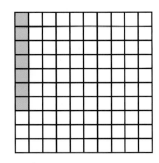

1.57

Next, eliminate the value of the subtrahead.

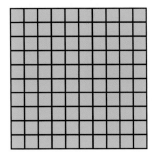 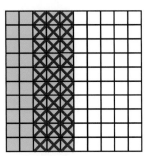 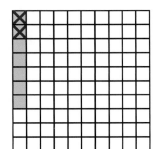

1.57
–0.32

To find the **difference**, add together what is remaining.

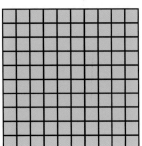 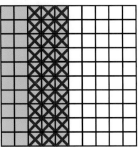 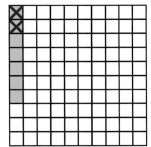

1.☺☺
0.2☺
+0.05
_____
1.25

What is the subtraction problem and answer for each model?

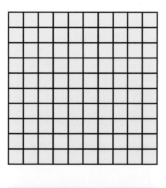 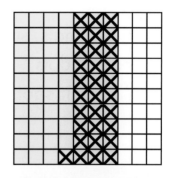

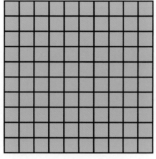 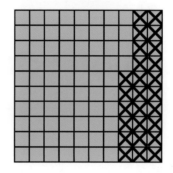

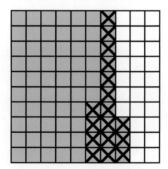

 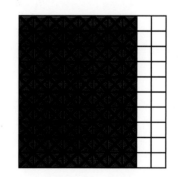

When subtracting decimals, subtract as usual,
but keep those decimal dots
lined up correctly in their spot.

Subtract: 1.06 from 2.8

2.8☺
-1.06
———
1.74

Annexing zeros to the right does not change the value: It means there are zero hundredths or thousandths.

Find each difference. Remember to include the decimal point in your answer!

20.75 – 16

16.5 – 8.6

0.1 – 0.01

998.8 – 18.31

32 – 0.09

Multiply Decimals

Crossover models will help you see
how multiplying decimals shrinks them instantly.

Let's take a peek at a model to find

$$0.3 \times 0.4$$

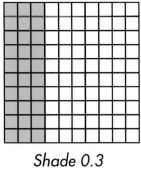

Shade 0.3
Vertically

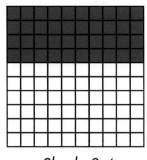

Shade 0.4
Horizontally

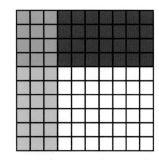

Count the overlapped part
to find the product

$$0.3 \times 0.4 = 0.12$$

As you can see, the **product** 0.12 is smaller than each **factor**.

Repeated addition is the best situation
to model whole number and decimal multiplication.

Let's see how to find 0.3 **of** 3 instantly!

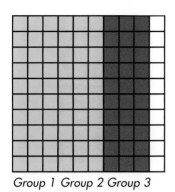

Group 1 Group 2 Group 3

To find the product, add each group together.

3 × 0.3 = 0.9

Find the multiplication problem and product for each model.

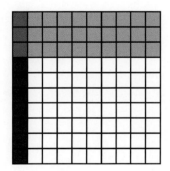
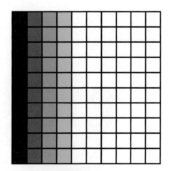
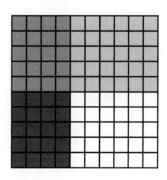

Either answer is correct thanks to the **commutative property of multiplication.**

Answers:

0.1 × 0.3 = 0.03 or
0.3 × 0.1 = 0.03

4 × 0.1 = 0.4 or
0.1 × 4 - 0.4

0.5 × 0.4 = 0.20

Multiplying decimals is really cool.
No need to line up decimals,
just multiply as usual is the rule.

Once you are through, the number
of decimal places in the product
must equal the total number of
decimal places in the factors.

$$
\begin{array}{r}
3{.}98 \\
\times\,7{.}4 \\
\hline
1592 \\
+\,27860 \\
\hline
29{,}452
\end{array}
$$

3 Total

3 Total

If a product runs short of spots,
annex zeros so the decimal dot
can find its spot.

$$
\begin{array}{r}
0{.}43 \\
\times\,0{.}06 \\
\hline
\odot 258
\end{array}
$$

4 3 2 1

Check It Out!

Always estimate to be sure
your decimal dot has landed
in the correct spot.
3.98 is about 4
7.4 is about 7
7 × 4 = 28
29.452 is close to 28, so the
decimal dot was placed in
the correct spot!

How many places over will the decimal be in the product?

$$0.75 \times 0.02$$

$$2.86 \times 4.37$$

$$1.34 \times 9.8$$

$$2.4 \times 1.2$$

$$2.4 \times 5$$

Multiply by Decimal Powers of 10

Discover the pattern of multiplying by powers of 10.
It gives you the ability to solve problems mentally.
This is great news and is based on just a few simple rules.

First, count the number of decimal places in the power of 10.

0.1   One Spot
0.01   Two Spots
0.001   Three Spots

To solve mentally, move the decimal point one place to the left for each decimal place in the decimal power of 10.

0.1 × 253 = 25.3   Move the decimal one spot to the left.
0.01 × 253 = 2.53   Move the decimal two spots to the left.
0.001 × 253 = 0.253 Move the decimal three spots to the left.

If a product runs short of spots,
annex zeros, so the decimal dot
can find its spot.

$$0.01 \times 4.5 = 0.045$$

Solve each product mentally.

32.1 × 0.01

12 × 0.001

0.59 × 0.1

12.8 × 0.001

352 × 0.1

0.7 × 0.01

Divide Decimals

Dividing a decimal by a whole number is simple to do. The first step is to move the decimal dot straight up from the **dividend** to mark its spot in the **quotient**. Once the decimal dot finds it's new spot, divide as usual.

$$
\begin{array}{r}
\textbf{1.32} \\
7\,\overline{)\,9.24\,} \\
\end{array}
$$

Quotient

Divisor

Dividend

```
        1.32    Quotient
Divisor 7)9.24  Dividend
       -7
       ——
        22
       -21
       ———
         14
        -14
        ———
          0
```

Decimals Replace Remainders

Instead of leaving a **remainder**, annex zeros until the remainder is gone.

```
        15.125
   8 ) 121.000
       -8
       ‾‾
        41
       -40
       ‾‾‾
         10
         -8
         ‾‾
         20
        -16
        ‾‾‾
          40
         -40
         ‾‾‾
           0
```

If the quotient begins to repeat,
use bar notation over the repeating digits.

```
       36.6̄66
   3 ) 110.000
       -9
       ‾‾
        20
       -18
       ‾‾‾
         20
        -18
        ‾‾‾
          20
         -18
         ‾‾‾
           20
```

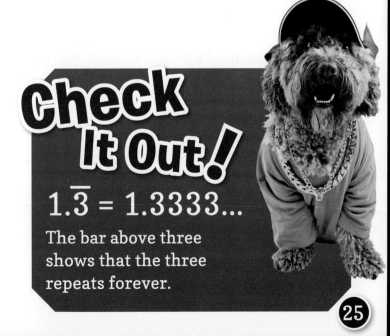

Check It Out!

$1.\overline{3} = 1.3333...$

The bar above three shows that the three repeats forever.

Divide Decimals by Decimals

Decimal division is never done.

Before you begin, turn the **divisor** into a whole number by shifting the decimal point all the way to the right.

$$.05\overline{)1.5}$$

Shift the decimal to the right in the dividend the same number of places. Annex zeros if needed.

Move the decimal dot straight up to mark its spot in the quotient.

$$5 \overline{)15\odot.}$$

Divide as usual.

$$
\begin{array}{r}
30. \\
5 \overline{)15\odot.} \\
-15 \\
\hline
00
\end{array}
$$

$$1.5 \div .05 = 30$$

Divide by Decimal Powers of 10

Discovering the pattern of dividing by powers of 10,
gives you the ability to solve problems mentally.
This is great news and is based on just a few simple rules.

First, shift the decimal in the power of 10 until it becomes the
number one.

0.1   One Spot

0.01   Two Spots

0.001   Three Spots

To solve mentally, shift the decimal point in the dividend the same
number of places. If the quotient runs short of spots, annex zeros so
the decimal dot can find its spot.

0.68 ÷ 0.01 = 68   Shift the decimal dot two spots.
7.22 ÷ 0.1 = 72.2   Shift the decimal dot one spot.
84 ÷ 0.001 = 84,000   Shift the decimal dot three spots.

Find each quotient mentally.

28 ÷ 0.1

0.585 ÷ 0.01

8.03 ÷ 0.001

4.12 ÷ 0.1

Glossary

addends (AD-ends): the numbers that are added together in an addition problem

annex (an-EKS): to place zeros at the beginning or end of a decimal

commutative property of multiplication (kuh-MYOO-tuh-tiv PROP-ur-tee uhv muhl-tuh-pli-KEY-shuhn): if the order or the factors change, the product remains the same

denominators (di-NOM-uh-nay-torz): the bottom numbers of a fraction that shows the number of equal parts of the whole

difference (DIF-ur-uhnss): the answer to a subtraction problem

digit (DIJ-it): a written symbol for any numbers 0 to 9

dividend (DIV-i-dend): the number being divided up in a division problem

divisor (di-VYE-zur): the number being divided by in a division problem

factor (FAK-tur): the number or numbers that are multiplied

minuend (MIN-yoo-end): the number being subtracted in a subtraction problem

product (PROD-uhkt): the answer to a multiplication problem

quotient (KWOH-shuhnt): the answer to a division problem

remainder (ri-MAYN-dur): the number left over when numbers do not divide equally

sum (suhm): the answer to an addition problem

Index

Websites to Visit

www.coolmath-games.com/decimals-cruncher/
  decimals-cruncher-multiplication.htm

www.mrnussbaum.com/lunchlady-play

www.mathnook.com/math/bubbleburst.html

About the Author

Lisa Arias is a math teacher who lives in Tampa, Florida with her husband and two children. Her out-of-the-box thinking and love for math guided her toward becoming an author. She enjoys playing board games and spending time with family and friends.

Meet The Author!
www.meetREMauthors.com

PHOTO CREDITS: Cover: © DvdArts, CactuSoup, JulyVelchev, leysan; Page 13: © owncham

Edited by: Jill Sherman

Cover and Interior design by: Tara Raymo

Library of Congress PCN Data

Dazzling Decimals: Decimals and Fractions / Lisa Arias
(Got Math!)
ISBN 978-1-62717-714-6 (hard cover)
ISBN 978-1-62717-836-5 (soft cover)
ISBN 978-1-62717-949-2 (e-Book)
Library of Congress Control Number: 2014935591

Printed in the United States of America, North Mankato, Minnesota

Also Available as: